HEAVEN'S WHISPER

A 30-Day Prophetic Prayer Devotional

JAUN MALCOLM

EDITED BY
NICOLE QUEEN

VISION PUBLISHING
HOUSE

All rights reserved. Published in the United States by Vision Publishing House.

Vision Publishing House
www.vision-publishinghouse.com
support@vision-publishinghouse.com

ISBN: 978-1-955297-83-7
LCCN: 2025902823

This book is established to provide information and inspiration to all readers. It is designed with the understanding that the author is not engaged to render any psychological, legal, or any other kind of professional advice. The content is the sole expression of the author. The author is not liable for any physical, psychological, emotional, financial, or commercial damages, including, but not limited to special, incidental, consequential, or other damages. All readers are responsible for their own choices, actions, and results.

To those who have felt lost in the noise of the world, unsure of their purpose, and yearning for deeper connection— may you find comfort, clarity, and peace in His whisper...

"After the earthquake came a fire, but the Lord was not in the fire. And after the fire came a gentle whisper."

— 1 KINGS 19:12

CONTENTS

INTRODUCTION

In a world full of noise, chaos, and constant distractions, it can be easy to feel disconnected from God's presence. The busyness of life pulls us in every direction, and we often find ourselves yearning for clarity, peace, and a deeper connection with the One who created us. But here's the truth: God is always speaking. The question is: *are we listening?*

Heaven's Whisper was born out of a desire to help you tune into the gentle, loving voice of God amidst the clamor of everyday life. This devotional isn't just about reading Scripture or reciting prayers; it's about cultivating a posture of stillness, attentiveness, and intimacy with the Father. When we quiet our hearts and lean into His presence, we discover that His voice has been there all along—guiding, comforting, and aligning us with His perfect will.

Over the next 30 days, you'll embark on a journey of spiritual renewal and transformation. Each day is thoughtfully structured to help you:

- Engage with *The Sword* – the powerful Word of God that cuts through confusion and fights off evil.
- Reflect with *The Armor* – personal insights and applications that encourage you to internalize and live out the truth of Scripture, while equipping yourself with the full Armor of God: the Belt of Truth, the Breastplate of Righteousness, the Shoes of Peace, the Shield of Faith, the Helmet of Salvation, and the Sword of the Spirit.

- Pray with *The Shield* – heartfelt prayers that draw you into deeper communion with God, fortifying your spirit against life's challenges, and extinguishes the flaming arrows of evil.
- Journal Your Journey – capturing your reflections, revelations, and prayers as you grow in faith and understanding.

Before we journey together, please remember that this isn't a race to the finish line. It's an invitation to *slow down*, be still, and embrace the beauty of God's whisper in your life. As you commit to this time of devotion, expect God to meet you in profound ways—shaping your thoughts, transforming your heart, and aligning your steps with His purpose.

May *Heaven's Whisper* lead you into deeper intimacy with the Lord, and may you come to know His voice as the guiding force in every area of your life.

* * *

Let the journey begin.

HOW TO USE THIS BOOK

 Call to Me, and I will answer you, and show you great and mighty things, which you do not know.

— JEREMIAH 33:3 (NKJV)

Heaven's Whisper was designed to be more than just a daily prayer devotional—it's an invitation to deepen your relationship with God, hear His voice clearly, and walk in alignment with His will. Each day's reading will guide you into a rhythm of Scripture, reflection, and prayer, helping you cultivate a lifestyle of intimacy with the Lord.

Here's how to engage with this prayer devotional:

1. Find a Quiet Space: Begin each day by setting aside a quiet moment with God. Eliminate distractions and create an atmosphere where you can focus on His presence—whether it's in the morning, during a lunch break, or before bed. Approach each day with expectation, knowing that God desires to speak to you.

2. Engage with The Sword: Each day starts with *The Sword*, which is a Scripture that anchors the devotional. Read it slowly, meditate on its meaning, and let it sink into your heart. Consider reading it aloud to help the words resonate deeply within you.

3. Reflect with The Armor: After reading the Scripture, move into *The Armor*, a reflection that unpacks the verse and applies it to your life. This section is designed to equip you spiritually by applying biblical truths to your life. Just as the Armor of God protects and empowers believers, these reflections help you stand firm in faith. As you read, allow the *Belt of Truth* to ground you in God's Word, the *Helmet of Salvation* to remind you of your identity in Christ, and the *Shoes of Peace* to guide you in walking with confidence and trust in Him.

4. Pray with The Shield: Close each day with *The Shield*, a prayer crafted to help you connect with God on a deeper level. Feel free to use the written prayer as a starting point, but also let your own words flow. This is your sacred time to commune with the Lord—pour out your heart and listen for His whisper.

5. Journal Your Journey: After each devotional, take time to journal. Use the prompts provided to guide your reflections, but don't limit yourself. Write down any personal revelations, prayers, or insights God places on your heart. This space is for you to document your spiritual growth, struggles, and victories. Over time, you'll be able to look back and see how God has been moving in your life.

6. Go at Your Own Pace: While this devotional is structured for daily use, don't feel pressured to rush through it. If a particular day's message speaks to you deeply, linger there. Let God lead you through this journey at the pace that's right for you.

7. Approach with Expectation: God desires to speak to you more than you desire to hear from Him. As you move through *Heaven's Whisper*, come with an open heart and expect to encounter His presence. His voice might come as a gentle nudge, a sudden clarity, or through the words of Scripture—but rest assured, He is speaking.

* * *

Before we begin, let's take some time to pause and reflect.

- What is God whispering to your heart today?
- How does Jeremiah 33:3 speak to your current season of life?
- In what ways can you create more space to hear God's voice?

Take a deep breath, open your heart, and prepare to hear from Heaven. This is your sacred space to draw near to God and experience His presence in new and transformative ways. Use the space below to journal your thoughts, prayers, and reflections before we begin.

Let this be a foundational space that aligns your focus throughout this journey, giving you a place to return whenever you need to reconnect with why you started.

* * *

1. What is God whispering to your heart today?

_____
_____
_____
_____
_____
_____
_____
_____
_____
_____
_____
_____
_____
_____
_____
_____
_____
_____
_____
_____
_____
_____
_____
_____
_____
_____
_____
_____
_____

2. How does Jeremiah 33:3 speak to your current season of life?

_____

_____

_____

_____

_____

_____

_____

_____

_____

_____

_____

_____

_____

_____

_____

_____

_____

_____

_____

_____

_____

_____

_____

_____

_____

_____

_____

_____

_____

_____

_____

_____

3. In what ways can you create more space to hear God's voice?

_____

_____

_____

_____

_____

_____

_____

_____

_____

_____

_____

_____

_____

_____

_____

_____

_____

_____

_____

_____

_____

_____

_____

_____

DAY 1

AWAKENING TO HIS PRESENCE

SWORD OF THE SPIRIT

"Draw near to God, and He will draw near to you." —James 4:8 (NKJV)

FULL ARMOR OF GOD

The first step to encountering God's voice is to draw near to Him. You have a part to play in connecting with God. It will require dedication and discipline to step into the place of prayer where you will not just sense His presence, but feel Him hold you in His hands. God desires intimacy with you. When you approach Him with an open heart, He promises to meet you where you are. The Holy Spirit is always present, but we must actively position ourselves to listen. *Are you aware of God's presence in your life?*

SHIELD OF FAITH

Lord, I draw near to You today. I intentionally pull away from the distractions of this world just to be close to You. Help me to tune my heart to Your voice so I may discern when You are speaking to me. Open my eyes to Your presence in every moment. I desire to know You more intimately. Speak to me today Lord, and help me hear You clearly.

In Jesus name I pray, Amen.

1. How do you currently recognize God's presence in your daily life?

_____

_____

_____

_____

_____

_____

_____

_____

2. What distractions do you need to set aside to draw nearer to Him?

_____

_____

_____

_____

_____

_____

_____

_____

_____

3. Describe a time when you felt God holding you in His hands.

_____

_____

_____

_____

_____

_____

_____

_____

Whispers from the Heart

This space is for your heart's dialogue with God. Whether it's a prayer, a reflection, a question, or a moment of gratitude—allow this area to capture what God is revealing to you in your journey. There are no rules here, just an open invitation to pour out your thoughts and listen for His whisper— from the One who knows you best.

_____
_____
_____
_____
_____
_____
_____
_____
_____
_____
_____
_____
_____
_____
_____
_____
_____
_____
_____
_____
_____
_____
_____
_____
_____

DAY 2

IDENTITY IN CHRIST

SWORD OF THE SPIRIT

"You are a chosen generation, a royal priesthood, a holy nation, His own special people, that you may proclaim the praises of Him who called you out of darkness into His marvelous light." — 1 Peter 2:9 (NKJV)

FULL ARMOR OF GOD

You are God's chosen vessel, created in His image and likeness. You are precious in His sight. As you begin this journey, remember your identity in Christ. The enemy works tirelessly to keep you from the knowledge of God and who you are in Him. The enemy may try to tell you otherwise, but your worth and value are defined by God, not the world. You have been set apart for His glory. You are not a mistake, you were created on purpose. *Who are you in Christ?*

SHIELD OF FAITH

Father, thank You for choosing me. Thank You that my past does not disqualify me from my destiny. Thank You for snatching me from the doors of destruction and pulling me into Your light. Who I was is not who I am today. Help me to see myself through Your eyes and walk in the fullness of my identity in Christ. Let me always remember that I am loved, chosen, and set apart for Your purposes. Empower me to live as your royal priesthood and holy nation today.

In Jesus name I pray, Amen.

* * *

1. How has knowing you are chosen by God changed your perspective on life?

_____
_____
_____
_____
_____
_____
_____

2. What lies has the enemy tried to make you believe about your identity?

_____
_____
_____
_____
_____
_____
_____

3. Write a declaration of who you are in Christ today.

_____
_____
_____
_____
_____
_____
_____

Whispers from the Heart

This space is for your heart's dialogue with God. Whether it's a prayer, a reflection, a question, or a moment of gratitude—allow this area to capture what God is revealing to you in your journey. There are no rules here, just an open invitation to pour out your thoughts and listen for His whisper— from the One who knows you best.

_____

_____

_____

_____

_____

_____

_____

_____

_____

_____

_____

_____

_____

_____

_____

_____

_____

_____

_____

_____

_____

_____

_____

_____

_____

DAY 3

GOD'S VOICE IN THE SILENCE

SWORD OF THE SPIRIT

"Be still, and know that I am God." – Psalm 46:10 (NIV)

FULL ARMOR OF GOD

In the quiet, God's voice often becomes clearer. Though, at times, it seems chaotic all around you, practice silence. The world can easily distract and call us away from His presence but take a deep breath and exhale. Yes, the world is loud, but in the stillness, we can hear Him more distinctly. Set aside time each day to be silent before God and allow His voice to resonate in your heart. Sometimes, silence is where we hear the deepest revelations. *What's the biggest obstacle for you to hear God's voice?*

SHIELD OF FAITH

Lord, I come before You in stillness today. I shut off the voices of the world and incline my ears to hear Your instructions. I quiet my soul and open my heart to receive You. Reveal yourself to me in the silence. Teach me to discern Your whispers in my life.

In Jesus name I pray, Amen.

1. When was the last time you experienced God's voice in silence?

_____
_____
_____
_____
_____
_____
_____
_____
_____

2. What are the biggest obstacles keeping you from being still before God?

_____
_____
_____
_____
_____
_____
_____
_____
_____

3. How can you create more intentional moments of silence in your life?

_____
_____
_____
_____
_____
_____
_____
_____
_____

Whispers from the Heart

This space is for your heart's dialogue with God. Whether it's a prayer, a reflection, a question, or a moment of gratitude—allow this area to capture what God is revealing to you in your journey. There are no rules here, just an open invitation to pour out your thoughts and listen for His whisper— from the One who knows you best.

_____
_____
_____
_____
_____
_____
_____
_____
_____
_____
_____
_____
_____
_____
_____
_____
_____
_____
_____
_____
_____
_____
_____
_____
_____
_____

DAY 4

STRENGTH FOR THE JOURNEY

SWORD OF THE SPIRIT

"I can do all things through Christ who strengthens me." – Philippians 4:13 (NKJV)

FULL ARMOR OF GOD

God equips you for the journey ahead. In moments of weakness or uncertainty, remember that He is your source of strength. Through Him, you can overcome every obstacle. When you align yourself with His promises, every mountain before you will have to come down. Trust that His power is at work within you, enabling you to accomplish all He has called you to do. *How has God shown His strength in your life?*

SHIELD OF FAITH

Lord, You are the God of the impossible! I thank You for being my source of strength. When I feel weak, remind me that Your power is made perfect in my weakness. I put my trust in You knowing that You will empower me to fulfill Your calling on my life. I ask that You strengthen me for the journey ahead. Get the glory out of my life.

In Jesus name I pray, Amen.

1. Describe a moment when God gave you strength in your weakness.

_____

_____

_____

_____

_____

_____

_____

_____

_____

2. What challenges are you facing that require God's strength today?

_____

_____

_____

_____

_____

_____

_____

_____

_____

3. How do you see God preparing you for the journey ahead?

_____

_____

_____

_____

_____

_____

_____

_____

Whispers from the Heart

This space is for your heart's dialogue with God. Whether it's a prayer, a reflection, a question, or a moment of gratitude—allow this area to capture what God is revealing to you in your journey. There are no rules here, just an open invitation to pour out your thoughts and listen for His whisper— from the One who knows you best.

_____

_____

_____

_____

_____

_____

_____

_____

_____

_____

_____

_____

_____

_____

_____

_____

_____

_____

_____

_____

_____

_____

_____

_____

_____

_____

DAY 5

RENEWING YOUR MIND

SWORD OF THE SPIRIT

"Do not be conformed to this world, but be transformed by the renewing of your mind, that you may prove what is that good and acceptable and perfect will of God." – Romans 12:2 (NKJV)

FULL ARMOR OF GOD

The battlefield for your soul is often in your mind. To hear God's voice clearly, you must allow Him to transform your thoughts. This renewal process involves surrendering old mindsets, false beliefs, and worldly perspectives. Unsubscribe from the noise of the world and those who are spiritually blind. Come out of agreement with belief systems that are contrary to God's word. *How have you allowed God's truth to guide your thoughts?*

SHIELD OF FAITH

Father, I surrender my thoughts to You today. Transform my mind by the power of Your Word. Remove any lies I have believed and replace them with Your truth. Help me to think the way You think. I will train my thoughts to think on good things and align my will with Your will for my life.

In Jesus name I pray, Amen.

17

1. What old mindsets or beliefs do you need to surrender to God today?

_____

_____

_____

_____

_____

_____

_____

_____

_____

_____

2. How has God's truth transformed your thoughts recently?

_____

_____

_____

_____

_____

_____

_____

_____

_____

_____

3. What Scriptures help you renew your mind when negative thoughts arise?

_____

_____

_____

_____

_____

_____

_____

_____

_____

WHISPERS FROM THE HEART

This space is for your heart's dialogue with God. Whether it's a prayer, a reflection, a question, or a moment of gratitude—allow this area to capture what God is revealing to you in your journey. There are no rules here, just an open invitation to pour out your thoughts and listen for His whisper— from the One who knows you best.

_____

_____

_____

_____

_____

_____

_____

_____

_____

_____

_____

_____

_____

_____

_____

_____

_____

_____

_____

_____

_____

_____

_____

_____

_____

_____

DAY 6

FAITH IN GOD'S PROMISES

SWORD OF THE SPIRIT

"For all the promises of God in Him are Yes, and in Him Amen, to the glory of God through us." – 2 Corinthians 1:20 (NKJV)

FULL ARMOR OF GOD

God is faithful to keep His promises. His Word will not return to Him void. No matter what your circumstances look like, hold fast to what God has spoken over your life. His promises are unshakeable, and He will bring them to pass. Prophetic prayer aligns your heart with His will, so trust in the certainty of His Word. *How can you exercise faith in God's promises in times of testing?*

SHIELD OF FAITH

Lord, thank you for your promises. I trust that You are faithful to fulfill all that You have spoken over my life. Help me to hold on to Your promises with unwavering faith. When my feet are unsteady help me to stand firm in Your promise over my life.

In Jesus name I pray, Amen.

1. What promises from God are you holding on to right now?

_____

_____

_____

_____

_____

_____

_____

_____

_____

_____

2. How can you strengthen your faith when His promises seem delayed?

_____

_____

_____

_____

_____

_____

_____

_____

_____

_____

3. Reflect on a time when God fulfilled a promise in your life.

_____

_____

_____

_____

_____

_____

_____

_____

_____

WHISPERS FROM THE HEART

This space is for your heart's dialogue with God. Whether it's a prayer, a reflection, a question, or a moment of gratitude—allow this area to capture what God is revealing to you in your journey. There are no rules here, just an open invitation to pour out your thoughts and listen for His whisper— from the One who knows you best.

_____

_____

_____

_____

_____

_____

_____

_____

_____

_____

_____

_____

_____

_____

_____

_____

_____

_____

_____

_____

_____

_____

_____

_____

_____

DAY 7

BREAKING STRONGHOLDS

SWORD OF THE SPIRIT

"For the weapons of our warfare are not carnal but mighty in God for pulling down strongholds." – 2 Corinthians 10:4 (NKJV)

FULL ARMOR OF GOD

There are spiritual strongholds that can hinder your connection to God. These could be lies, past hurts, or habits that keep you from fully walking in the freedom Christ offers. Through prayer, God can break these chains. Be bold and declare the victory of Christ over any area of your life that has been bound. *What are your strongholds?*

SHIELD OF FAITH

Lord, I ask You to reveal any strongholds in my life. Break every chain that binds me and set me free. I declare Your victory over every area of my mind, heart, and spirit. I trust in Your power to deliver and restore.

In Jesus name I pray, Amen.

1. What strongholds are you aware of that hinder your relationship with God?

_____

_____

_____

_____

_____

_____

_____

_____

2. How has God helped you overcome past strongholds in your life?

_____

_____

_____

_____

_____

_____

_____

_____

3. Write a prayer of declaration over the areas where you seek freedom.

_____

_____

_____

_____

_____

_____

_____

Whispers from the Heart

This space is for your heart's dialogue with God. Whether it's a prayer, a reflection, a question, or a moment of gratitude—allow this area to capture what God is revealing to you in your journey. There are no rules here, just an open invitation to pour out your thoughts and listen for His whisper— from the One who knows you best.

_____

_____

_____

_____

_____

_____

_____

_____

_____

_____

_____

_____

_____

_____

_____

_____

_____

_____

_____

_____

_____

_____

_____

_____

_____

_____

DAY 8

EMBRACING YOUR PURPOSE

SWORD OF THE SPIRIT

"For I know the plans I have for you, declares the Lord, plans for welfare and not for evil, to give you a future and a hope." – Jeremiah 29:11 (ESV)

FULL ARMOR OF GOD

God has a specific purpose for your life, and it is a good one. He created you for a reason, and He is working everything out to bring you into the fullness of your calling. Trust that His plans are greater than any plans you could make on your own. *How does your purpose align with God's purpose for your life?*

SHIELD OF FAITH

Father, I trust in Your perfect plan for my life. Help me to walk in my purpose with boldness and clarity. Lead me today in the steps You have ordained for me.

In Jesus name I pray, Amen.

1. What do you believe is your God-given purpose in this season of life?

_____
_____
_____
_____
_____
_____
_____
_____
_____
_____

2. How has God revealed His plans for you in the past?

_____
_____
_____
_____
_____
_____
_____
_____
_____
_____

3. What steps can you take today to align more closely with His purpose?

_____
_____
_____
_____
_____
_____
_____
_____
_____

WHISPERS FROM THE HEART

This space is for your heart's dialogue with God. Whether it's a prayer, a reflection, a question, or a moment of gratitude—allow this area to capture what God is revealing to you in your journey. There are no rules here, just an open invitation to pour out your thoughts and listen for His whisper— from the One who knows you best.

_____

_____

_____

_____

_____

_____

_____

_____

_____

_____

_____

_____

_____

_____

_____

_____

_____

_____

_____

_____

_____

_____

_____

_____

_____

DAY 9

BREAKING FREE FROM FEAR

SWORD OF THE SPIRIT

"For God has not given us a spirit of fear, but of power and of love and of a sound mind."
– 2 Timothy 1:7 (NKJV)

FULL ARMOR OF GOD

Fear is a tool the enemy uses to keep you from stepping into your destiny. But God has equipped you with power, love, and a sound mind to overcome fear. As you pray today, release any fear that has been holding you back from fully trusting God and moving forward in faith. *In what areas of your life has fear kept you stagnant?*

SHIELD OF FAITH

Lord, I release every fear that has gripped my heart. I declare that I have the power to overcome fear because You are with me. Fill me with Your perfect love that casts out all fear. Empower me to walk in courage today.

In Jesus name I pray, Amen.

1. What fears have been holding you back from fully trusting God?

_____

_____

_____

_____

_____

_____

_____

_____

2. How has God helped you overcome fear in the past?

_____

_____

_____

_____

_____

_____

_____

_____

_____

3. Write a declaration of faith to replace fear with trust in God.

_____

_____

_____

_____

_____

_____

_____

_____

WHISPERS FROM THE HEART

This space is for your heart's dialogue with God. Whether it's a prayer, a reflection, a question, or a moment of gratitude—allow this area to capture what God is revealing to you in your journey. There are no rules here, just an open invitation to pour out your thoughts and listen for His whisper— from the One who knows you best.

_____

_____

_____

_____

_____

_____

_____

_____

_____

_____

_____

_____

_____

_____

_____

_____

_____

_____

_____

_____

_____

_____

_____

_____

_____

DAY 10

HEARING GOD'S VOICE CLEARLY

SWORD OF THE SPIRIT

"My sheep hear My voice, and I know them, and they follow Me." – John 10:27 (NKJV)

FULL ARMOR OF GOD

God speaks to His people, and if you are His, you can hear His voice. Prophetic prayer is all about tuning into God's voice. Sometimes, it's a whisper, other times it's a still small voice, and sometimes it's a bold declaration. Stay attuned to His leading, and practice listening in the quiet moments. *How do you know when God is speaking to you? How often do you follow what you hear?*

SHIELD OF FAITH

Lord, thank You that I can hear Your voice. I want to be more attuned to Your speaking in my life. Help me to recognize Your voice above all others. Speak to me clearly today, and guide my steps.

In Jesus name I pray, Amen.

1. How do you personally recognize when God is speaking to you?

_____

_____

_____

_____

_____

_____

_____

_____

_____

2. Reflect on a time when you followed God's voice and saw His hand move.

_____

_____

_____

_____

_____

_____

_____

_____

_____

3. What practices help you stay attuned to hearing God's voice clearly?

_____

_____

_____

_____

_____

_____

_____

_____

_____

Whispers from the Heart

This space is for your heart's dialogue with God. Whether it's a prayer, a reflection, a question, or a moment of gratitude—allow this area to capture what God is revealing to you in your journey. There are no rules here, just an open invitation to pour out your thoughts and listen for His whisper— from the One who knows you best.

_____

_____

_____

_____

_____

_____

_____

_____

_____

_____

_____

_____

_____

_____

_____

_____

_____

_____

_____

_____

_____

_____

_____

_____

_____

_____

DAY 11

INTIMACY WITH THE HOLY SPIRIT

SWORD OF THE SPIRIT

"But the Helper, the Holy Spirit, whom the Father will send in My name, He will teach you all things, and bring to your remembrance all things that I said to you." – John 14:26 (NKJV)

FULL ARMOR OF GOD

The Holy Spirit is your teacher, guide, and comforter. As you deepen your connection to God, invite the Holy Spirit to move in your life. He will lead you into all truth and empower you to fulfill your purpose. *What are some ways you can be intimate with the Holy Spirit?*

SHIELD OF FAITH

Holy Spirit, I welcome Your presence today. Teach me, guide me, and empower me to live in the fullness of God's will. Help me to hear Your voice and follow Your lead in every area of my life.

In Jesus name I pray, Amen.

1. How do you experience the Holy Spirit in your everyday life?

_____
_____
_____
_____
_____
_____
_____
_____
_____

2. What areas of your life are you inviting the Holy Spirit to lead?

_____
_____
_____
_____
_____
_____
_____
_____
_____

3. Write about a time when the Holy Spirit taught or comforted you.

_____
_____
_____
_____
_____
_____
_____
_____
_____

Whispers from the Heart

This space is for your heart's dialogue with God. Whether it's a prayer, a reflection, a question, or a moment of gratitude—allow this area to capture what God is revealing to you in your journey. There are no rules here, just an open invitation to pour out your thoughts and listen for His whisper— from the One who knows you best.

_____

_____

_____

_____

_____

_____

_____

_____

_____

_____

_____

_____

_____

_____

_____

_____

_____

_____

_____

_____

_____

_____

_____

_____

_____

_____

Day 12

Courage to Step into the Unknown

Sword of the Spirit

"Trust in the Lord with all your heart, and lean not on your own understanding; in all your ways acknowledge Him, and He shall direct your paths." – Proverbs 3:5-6 (NKJV)

Full Armor of God

God often calls us to step into the unknown— to trust Him with what we cannot see. The journey may be uncertain, but His direction is always clear. Have the courage to trust God fully and step out in faith, even when the path ahead seems unclear. *What are some areas in your life that you need to let go of to let God lead?*

Shield of Faith

Lord, I trust You with the unknowns in my life. Help me to step forward in faith, trusting that You will direct my steps. Give me the courage to follow You, even when I cannot see the whole picture.

In Jesus name I pray, Amen.

1. What unknowns in your life require you to trust God more fully?

_____
_____
_____
_____
_____
_____
_____
_____
_____

2. Describe a time when stepping out in faith led to a breakthrough.

_____
_____
_____
_____
_____
_____
_____
_____
_____

3. How can you lean not on your own understanding in this season?

_____
_____
_____
_____
_____
_____
_____
_____

WHISPERS FROM THE HEART

This space is for your heart's dialogue with God. Whether it's a prayer, a reflection, a question, or a moment of gratitude—allow this area to capture what God is revealing to you in your journey. There are no rules here, just an open invitation to pour out your thoughts and listen for His whisper— from the One who knows you best.

_____
_____
_____
_____
_____
_____
_____
_____
_____
_____
_____
_____
_____
_____
_____
_____
_____
_____
_____
_____
_____
_____
_____
_____

DAY 13

GOD'S TIMING IS PERFECT

SWORD OF THE SPIRIT

"He has made everything beautiful in its time." – Ecclesiastes 3:11 (NIV)

FULL ARMOR OF GOD

God operates outside of time, and His timing is always perfect. Whether you're waiting for a breakthrough, a promise to be fulfilled, or an answer to prayer, trust that God is never late. He is orchestrating everything in your life for His glory and your good. *What are some things you can do while waiting on God's timing?*

SHIELD OF FAITH

Lord, help me to trust in Your perfect timing. I surrender my impatience to You and rest in the assurance that You are working all things out for my good. Teach me to wait with hope and expectation.

In Jesus name I pray, Amen.

1. How do you respond when God's timing doesn't align with your own?

_____

_____

_____

_____

_____

_____

_____

_____

_____

_____

2. What is God teaching you in your current season of waiting?

_____

_____

_____

_____

_____

_____

_____

_____

_____

_____

3. Reflect on a time when you saw God's perfect timing unfold in your life.

_____

_____

_____

_____

_____

_____

_____

_____

_____

Whispers from the Heart

This space is for your heart's dialogue with God. Whether it's a prayer, a reflection, a question, or a moment of gratitude—allow this area to capture what God is revealing to you in your journey. There are no rules here, just an open invitation to pour out your thoughts and listen for His whisper— from the One who knows you best.

_____
_____
_____
_____
_____
_____
_____
_____
_____
_____
_____
_____
_____
_____
_____
_____
_____
_____
_____
_____
_____
_____
_____
_____
_____

Day 14

Walking in Authority

Sword of the Spirit

"Behold, I give you the authority to trample on serpents and scorpions, and over all the power of the enemy, and nothing shall by any means hurt you." – Luke 10:19 (NKJV)

Full Armor of God

God has given you authority as His child. You are not powerless; you have the authority to overcome the enemy and walk in victory. Walk in the boldness of that authority today, knowing that you have been equipped to stand firm in the face of opposition. *How can you demonstrate your authority in your daily life?*

Shield of Faith

Lord, thank You for the authority You've given me. I declare victory over every attack of the enemy in my life. I stand in the power of Your Name, knowing that I am victorious in You.

In Jesus name I pray, Amen.

1. What areas of your life do you need to walk in God-given authority?

_____

_____

_____

_____

_____

_____

_____

_____

_____

2. How has God equipped you to overcome spiritual battles?

_____

_____

_____

_____

_____

_____

_____

_____

_____

3. Write a declaration affirming the authority you have in Christ.

_____

_____

_____

_____

_____

_____

_____

_____

Whispers from the Heart

This space is for your heart's dialogue with God. Whether it's a prayer, a reflection, a question, or a moment of gratitude—allow this area to capture what God is revealing to you in your journey. There are no rules here, just an open invitation to pour out your thoughts and listen for His whisper— from the One who knows you best.

_____

_____

_____

_____

_____

_____

_____

_____

_____

_____

_____

_____

_____

_____

_____

_____

_____

_____

_____

_____

_____

_____

_____

_____

DAY 15

EMBRACING YOUR GOD GIVEN GIFTS

SWORD OF THE SPIRIT

"As each one has received a gift, minister it to one another, as good stewards of the manifold grace of God." – 1 Peter 4:10 (NKJV)

FULL ARMOR OF GOD

You have unique gifts that God has given you to serve others and advance His kingdom. Take time today to reflect on your gifts and how you can use them to bless those around you. Your calling is tied to the gifts He has entrusted to you. *How can you use your gifts to bless others?*

SHIELD OF FAITH

Father, thank You for the gifts You've placed within me. Help me to use them wisely and generously for Your kingdom. Show me how to serve others and glorify You through my gifts.

In Jesus name I pray, Amen.

1. What gifts has God entrusted to you, and how are you using them?

_____

_____

_____

_____

_____

_____

_____

_____

_____

2. How can you steward your gifts to serve others and glorify God?

_____

_____

_____

_____

_____

_____

_____

_____

_____

3. Write about a time when using your gifts made a difference in someone's life.

_____

_____

_____

_____

_____

_____

_____

_____

WHISPERS FROM THE HEART

This space is for your heart's dialogue with God. Whether it's a prayer, a reflection, a question, or a moment of gratitude—allow this area to capture what God is revealing to you in your journey. There are no rules here, just an open invitation to pour out your thoughts and listen for His whisper— from the One who knows you best.

DAY 16

RESTORING BROKENNESS

SWORD OF THE SPIRIT

"He heals the brokenhearted and binds up their wounds." – Psalm 147:3 (NIV)

FULL ARMOR OF GOD

God is the healer of broken hearts. Whatever pain or hurt you carry today, bring it to Him. Trust that God is able to restore and make whole the places in your heart that have been wounded. He is in the business of making all things new. *What areas of your life need healing?*

SHIELD OF FAITH

Lord, I bring my brokenness before You today. Heal my heart and restore the areas of my life that are hurting. Thank You for Your tender mercy and for binding up my wounds.

In Jesus name I pray, Amen.

1. What areas of your heart do you need to invite God to heal?

_____

_____

_____

_____

_____

_____

_____

_____

_____

2. Reflect on a time when God brought restoration to your life.

_____

_____

_____

_____

_____

_____

_____

_____

_____

3. How can you trust God with the parts of your story that still feel broken?

_____

_____

_____

_____

_____

_____

_____

_____

Whispers from the Heart

This space is for your heart's dialogue with God. Whether it's a prayer, a reflection, a question, or a moment of gratitude—allow this area to capture what God is revealing to you in your journey. There are no rules here, just an open invitation to pour out your thoughts and listen for His whisper— from the One who knows you best.

_____

_____

_____

_____

_____

_____

_____

_____

_____

_____

_____

_____

_____

_____

_____

_____

_____

_____

_____

_____

_____

_____

_____

_____

_____

_____

DAY 17

THE POWER OF PRAISE

SWORD OF THE SPIRIT

"But You are holy, enthroned in the praises of Israel." – Psalm 22:3 (NKJV)

FULL ARMOR OF GOD

Praise invites God's presence and releases power. As you praise Him today, expect God to move in mighty ways. When you lift your voice in worship, you create a throne for God to dwell in and act on your behalf. *How might daily praise impact your life?*

SHIELD OF FAITH

Lord, I lift my voice in praise today. I invite Your presence into my life, and I declare that You are worthy of all honor and glory. Let my praise be a weapon against the enemy and a sign of Your greatness.

In Jesus name I pray, Amen.

1. How has praise shifted your perspective during difficult times?

_____
_____
_____
_____
_____
_____
_____
_____
_____

2. What does it mean to you that God inhabits the praises of His people?

_____
_____
_____
_____
_____
_____
_____
_____
_____
_____

3. Write a personal praise to God for who He is and what He's done.

_____
_____
_____
_____
_____
_____
_____
_____
_____

Whispers from the Heart

This space is for your heart's dialogue with God. Whether it's a prayer, a reflection, a question, or a moment of gratitude—allow this area to capture what God is revealing to you in your journey. There are no rules here, just an open invitation to pour out your thoughts and listen for His whisper— from the One who knows you best.

_____
_____
_____
_____
_____
_____
_____
_____
_____
_____
_____
_____
_____
_____
_____
_____
_____
_____
_____
_____
_____
_____
_____
_____
_____
_____

DAY 18

HEALING THROUGH FORGIVENESS

SWORD OF THE SPIRIT

"And whenever you stand praying, if you have anything against anyone, forgive him, that your Father in heaven may also forgive you your trespasses." – Mark 11:25 (NKJV)

FULL ARMOR OF GOD

Forgiveness is key to walking in freedom. God has forgiven you, and He calls you to forgive others. If there is unforgiveness in your heart, allow God to heal those wounds. Forgiveness is not just for the other person; it's for your freedom. *Write a list of people who you need to forgive and pray for them. How can this action free you?*

SHIELD OF FAITH

Lord, I choose to forgive today. I release any bitterness or offense that I have held in my heart. Heal my wounds, and help me to walk in the freedom that forgiveness brings.

In Jesus name I pray, Amen.

1. Who do you need to forgive today to experience freedom?

_____

_____

_____

_____

_____

_____

_____

_____

_____

2. How has forgiving someone else brought healing to your heart?

_____

_____

_____

_____

_____

_____

_____

_____

_____

3. What steps can you take to release bitterness and walk in forgiveness?

_____

_____

_____

_____

_____

_____

_____

_____

_____

Whispers from the Heart

This space is for your heart's dialogue with God. Whether it's a prayer, a reflection, a question, or a moment of gratitude—allow this area to capture what God is revealing to you in your journey. There are no rules here, just an open invitation to pour out your thoughts and listen for His whisper— from the One who knows you best.

_____
_____
_____
_____
_____
_____
_____
_____
_____
_____
_____
_____
_____
_____
_____
_____
_____
_____
_____
_____
_____
_____
_____
_____
_____
_____

Day 19

Walking in the Spirit

Sword of the Spirit

"If we live in the Spirit, let us also walk in the Spirit." – Galatians 5:25 (NKJV)

Full Armor of God

Walking in the Spirit means allowing God to lead your every step. Today, invite the Holy Spirit to guide you in all that you do. As you walk in the Spirit, you will be empowered to live in accordance with God's will and bear fruit that lasts. *In what ways can surrendering to God produce good fruit in your life?*

Shield of Faith

Holy Spirit, guide me today. Lead me in every decision and action, and help me to live according to Your will. I want to walk in the fullness of Your presence and power.

In Jesus name I pray, Amen.

1. How do you recognize when you're walking in the Spirit vs. the flesh?

_____
_____
_____
_____
_____
_____
_____
_____
_____

2. What fruit of the Spirit do you want to see more of in your life?

_____
_____
_____
_____
_____
_____
_____
_____
_____

3. Write about a time when the Holy Spirit led you in an unexpected way.

_____
_____
_____
_____
_____
_____
_____
_____
_____

WHISPERS FROM THE HEART

This space is for your heart's dialogue with God. Whether it's a prayer, a reflection, a question, or a moment of gratitude—allow this area to capture what God is revealing to you in your journey. There are no rules here, just an open invitation to pour out your thoughts and listen for His whisper— from the One who knows you best.

DAY 20

VICTORY IN JESUS

SWORD OF THE SPIRIT

"But thanks be to God, who gives us the victory through our Lord Jesus Christ." – 1 Corinthians 15:57 (NKJV)

FULL ARMOR OF GOD

Victory is already yours in Christ. No matter what battle you face today, remember that Jesus has already secured your victory. Stand in that assurance and declare that you are more than a conqueror in Him. *What are some victories you are walking in today?*

SHIELD OF FAITH

Thank You, Jesus, for securing my victory. I stand firm in the truth that I am victorious in You. Help me to walk in that victory today— confident that You have overcome every obstacle.

In Jesus name I pray, Amen.

1. What battles has God already given you victory over?

_____

_____

_____

_____

_____

_____

_____

_____

_____

2. How can you stand firm in the victory Jesus has secured for you?

_____

_____

_____

_____

_____

_____

_____

_____

_____

3. Write a declaration of victory over a current challenge in your life.

_____

_____

_____

_____

_____

_____

_____

_____

_____

WHISPERS FROM THE HEART

This space is for your heart's dialogue with God. Whether it's a prayer, a reflection, a question, or a moment of gratitude—allow this area to capture what God is revealing to you in your journey. There are no rules here, just an open invitation to pour out your thoughts and listen for His whisper— from the One who knows you best.

DAY 21

THE UNFAILING LOVE OF GOD

SWORD OF THE SPIRIT

"But God demonstrates His own love toward us, in that while we were still sinners, Christ died for us." – Romans 5:8 (NKJV)

FULL ARMOR OF GOD

God's love is not based on your performance; it is unconditional. He loved you at your worst, and He continues to love you today. Nothing you do can separate you from His love. Rest in the truth that you are fully known and fully loved by God. *Do you truly believe in God's love for you? How does He demonstrate it?*

SHIELD OF FAITH

Father, thank You for loving me even when I didn't deserve it. Help me to receive Your love fully and to walk in the confidence that I am cherished by You. Let Your love transform me from the inside out so I may reflect it to others.

In Jesus name I pray, Amen.

1. How has God demonstrated His unfailing love in your life?

_____
_____
_____
_____
_____
_____
_____
_____
_____
_____

2. Do you struggle to believe in God's unconditional love? Why or why not?

_____
_____
_____
_____
_____
_____
_____
_____
_____
_____

3. Write a prayer of gratitude for the ways God's love has transformed you.

_____
_____
_____
_____
_____
_____
_____
_____
_____

Whispers from the Heart

This space is for your heart's dialogue with God. Whether it's a prayer, a reflection, a question, or a moment of gratitude—allow this area to capture what God is revealing to you in your journey. There are no rules here, just an open invitation to pour out your thoughts and listen for His whisper— from the One who knows you best.

_____

_____

_____

_____

_____

_____

_____

_____

_____

_____

_____

_____

_____

_____

_____

_____

_____

_____

_____

_____

_____

_____

_____

_____

_____

DAY 22

THE POWER OF YOUR WORDS

SWORD OF THE SPIRIT

"Death and life are in the power of the tongue, and those who love it will eat its fruit."
– Proverbs 18:21 (NKJV)

FULL ARMOR OF GOD

Your words carry weight in the spirit. Every word you speak either aligns with God's truth or with the enemy's lies. Speak life over yourself and others. Declare the promises of God, and watch as His word manifests in your life. *What are you speaking over yourself today?*

SHIELD OF FAITH

Father, help me to be mindful of my words. Let my speech align with Your truth and not with the enemy's deception. I reject negativity, doubt, and fear. I choose to declare life, healing, and victory. May my words reflect Your heart and bring glory to Your name.

In Jesus name I pray, Amen.

1. What words have you been speaking over yourself lately?

_____
_____
_____
_____
_____
_____
_____
_____
_____
_____

2. How can you be more intentional about speaking life and truth?

_____
_____
_____
_____
_____
_____
_____
_____
_____
_____

3. Write declarations of God's promises over your life and future.

_____
_____
_____
_____
_____
_____
_____
_____
_____

WHISPERS FROM THE HEART

This space is for your heart's dialogue with God. Whether it's a prayer, a reflection, a question, or a moment of gratitude—allow this area to capture what God is revealing to you in your journey. There are no rules here, just an open invitation to pour out your thoughts and listen for His whisper— from the One who knows you best.

Day 23

Strength in Weakness

Sword of the Spirit

"My grace is sufficient for you, for My strength is made perfect in weakness."
– 2 Corinthians 12:9 (NKJV)

Full Armor of God

God is not looking for perfection; He is looking for surrender. When you feel weak, inadequate, or unqualified, that is where His strength is perfected. Trust Him to fill in the gaps and equip you for every good work. *Where do you need His strength today?*

Shield of Faith

Lord, I lay down my weaknesses before You. I acknowledge that I cannot do this on my own, but I trust in Your strength. Fill me with Your grace and power. Help me to walk in confidence, knowing that You are my source of strength.

In Jesus name I pray, Amen.

1. In what areas do you feel weak and in need of God's strength today?

_____

_____

_____

_____

_____

_____

_____

_____

_____

_____

2. How has God's grace been sufficient for you in past struggles?

_____

_____

_____

_____

_____

_____

_____

_____

_____

_____

3. Write about a time when God's strength carried you through.

_____

_____

_____

_____

_____

_____

_____

_____

_____

Whispers from the Heart

This space is for your heart's dialogue with God. Whether it's a prayer, a reflection, a question, or a moment of gratitude—allow this area to capture what God is revealing to you in your journey. There are no rules here, just an open invitation to pour out your thoughts and listen for His whisper— from the One who knows you best.

_____
_____
_____
_____
_____
_____
_____
_____
_____
_____
_____
_____
_____
_____
_____
_____
_____
_____
_____
_____
_____
_____
_____
_____
_____

DAY 24

PERFECT LOVE CASTS OUT FEAR

SWORD OF THE SPIRIT

"There is no fear in love; but perfect love casts out fear, because fear involves torment. But he who fears has not been made perfect in love." – 1 John 4:18 (NKJV)

FULL ARMOR OF GOD

Fear loses its grip when you abide in the love of God. His perfect love drives out anxiety, worry, and doubt. When you understand how deeply you are loved, fear no longer has authority over your life. *How are you allowing God's love to cast out your fears?*

SHIELD OF FAITH

Lord, I renounce fear and embrace Your perfect love. Fill every area of my heart with Your presence, so that fear has no place in me. Let me rest in the security of Your unfailing love and walk in boldness.

In Jesus name I pray, Amen.

1. How are you allowing God's perfect love to replace fear in your life?

_____

_____

_____

_____

_____

_____

_____

_____

_____

2. Reflect on a time when God's love gave you courage in a fearful situation.

_____

_____

_____

_____

_____

_____

_____

_____

_____

3. What fears do you need to surrender to God's love today?

_____

_____

_____

_____

_____

_____

_____

_____

WHISPERS FROM THE HEART

This space is for your heart's dialogue with God. Whether it's a prayer, a reflection, a question, or a moment of gratitude—allow this area to capture what God is revealing to you in your journey. There are no rules here, just an open invitation to pour out your thoughts and listen for His whisper— from the One who knows you best.

_____

_____

_____

_____

_____

_____

_____

_____

_____

_____

_____

_____

_____

_____

_____

_____

_____

_____

_____

_____

_____

_____

_____

_____

_____

_____

DAY 25

A HEART OF WORSHIP

SWORD OF THE SPIRIT

"God is Spirit, and those who worship Him must worship in spirit and truth." – John 4:24 (NKJV)

FULL ARMOR OF GOD

Worship is more than a song, it's a posture of the heart. True worship flows from intimacy with the Father. When you worship in spirit and truth, strongholds break, chains fall, and heaven responds. *What is your heart's posture in worship?*

SHIELD OF FAITH

Lord, I give You my worship— not just with my lips, but with my life. Let my heart be a dwelling place for Your presence. Teach me to worship You in spirit and in truth, that I may glorify You in all that I do.

In Jesus name I pray, Amen.

1. How does worship shift your focus from your problems to God's presence?

_____

_____

_____

_____

_____

_____

_____

_____

_____

2. What does it mean to you to worship in spirit and truth?

_____

_____

_____

_____

_____

_____

_____

_____

_____

3. Write a personal song or prayer of worship to God.

_____

_____

_____

_____

_____

_____

_____

_____

WHISPERS FROM THE HEART

This space is for your heart's dialogue with God. Whether it's a prayer, a reflection, a question, or a moment of gratitude—allow this area to capture what God is revealing to you in your journey. There are no rules here, just an open invitation to pour out your thoughts and listen for His whisper— from the One who knows you best.

_____

_____

_____

_____

_____

_____

_____

_____

_____

_____

_____

_____

_____

_____

_____

_____

_____

_____

_____

_____

_____

_____

_____

_____

_____

_____

_____

_____

DAY 26

FEAR HAS NO HOLD

SWORD OF THE SPIRIT

"For God has not given us a spirit of fear, but of power and of love and of a sound mind."
– 2 Timothy 1:7 (NKJV)

FULL ARMOR OF GOD

Fear is not from God. The enemy uses fear to paralyze and distract you from your calling. But you have been given power, love, and a sound mind. Stand firm and refuse to let fear dictate your life. *What fear do you need to surrender to God today?*

SHIELD OF FAITH

Father, I reject the spirit of fear. I receive Your power, love, and sound mind. Fear will not control me. I walk in faith, knowing that You are with me. Strengthen me to trust You completely.

In Jesus name I pray, Amen.

1. What fears have been trying to take hold of your heart recently?

_____

_____

_____

_____

_____

_____

_____

_____

_____

2. How can you stand firm in the power, love, and sound mind God has given you?

_____

_____

_____

_____

_____

_____

_____

_____

_____

3. Write a declaration of freedom from fear, trusting in God's promises.

_____

_____

_____

_____

_____

_____

_____

_____

Whispers from the Heart

This space is for your heart's dialogue with God. Whether it's a prayer, a reflection, a question, or a moment of gratitude—allow this area to capture what God is revealing to you in your journey. There are no rules here, just an open invitation to pour out your thoughts and listen for His whisper— from the One who knows you best.

_____
_____
_____
_____
_____
_____
_____
_____
_____
_____
_____
_____
_____
_____
_____
_____
_____
_____
_____
_____
_____
_____
_____
_____
_____

DAY 27

THE LORD IS YOUR SHEPHERD

SWORD OF THE SPIRIT

"The Lord is my shepherd; I shall not want." – Psalm 23:1 (NKJV)

FULL ARMOR OF GOD

God is your provider, protector, and guide. He leads you beside still waters and restores your soul. No matter what you face, He is faithful to care for you. *In what ways do you trust Him as your Shepherd?*

SHIELD OF FAITH

Lord, thank You for being my Shepherd. I trust You to lead, provide, and protect me. Even when I walk through dark valleys, I know You are with me. Help me to rest in Your presence.

In Jesus name I pray, Amen.

1. How has God guided, provided, or protected you recently?

_____

_____

_____

_____

_____

_____

_____

_____

_____

2. In what areas of your life do you need to trust God more as your Shepherd?

_____

_____

_____

_____

_____

_____

_____

_____

_____

_____

3. Reflect on a time when God restored your soul in a difficult season.

_____

_____

_____

_____

_____

_____

_____

_____

_____

WHISPERS FROM THE HEART

This space is for your heart's dialogue with God. Whether it's a prayer, a reflection, a question, or a moment of gratitude—allow this area to capture what God is revealing to you in your journey. There are no rules here, just an open invitation to pour out your thoughts and listen for His whisper— from the One who knows you best.

_____

_____

_____

_____

_____

_____

_____

_____

_____

_____

_____

_____

_____

_____

_____

_____

_____

_____

_____

_____

_____

_____

_____

_____

Day 28

The Battle Belongs to the Lord

Sword of the Spirit

"The Lord will fight for you, and you shall hold your peace." – Exodus 14:14 (NKJV)

Full Armor of God

The battles you face are not yours to fight alone. God is your defender. Stand firm in faith, and let Him move on your behalf. Victory is found in surrendering the fight to Him. *Are you trying to fight battles that belong to God?*

Shield of Faith

Father, I release my battles into Your hands. I will not strive in my own strength but trust in Your power. Fight for me, Lord, and let Your will be done.

In Jesus name I pray, Amen.

1. Are there battles you're fighting in your own strength instead of trusting God?

_____
_____
_____
_____
_____
_____
_____
_____
_____
_____

2. How can you surrender control and let God fight for you?

_____
_____
_____
_____
_____
_____
_____
_____
_____
_____

3. Write a prayer releasing your battles to the Lord.

_____
_____
_____
_____
_____
_____
_____
_____
_____

Whispers from the Heart

This space is for your heart's dialogue with God. Whether it's a prayer, a reflection, a question, or a moment of gratitude—allow this area to capture what God is revealing to you in your journey. There are no rules here, just an open invitation to pour out your thoughts and listen for His whisper— from the One who knows you best.

_____

_____

_____

_____

_____

_____

_____

_____

_____

_____

_____

_____

_____

_____

_____

_____

_____

_____

_____

_____

_____

_____

_____

_____

_____

_____

DAY 29

A NEW CREATION

SWORD OF THE SPIRIT

"Therefore, if anyone is in Christ, he is a new creation; old things have passed away; behold, all things have become new." – 2 Corinthians 5:17 (NKJV)

FULL ARMOR OF GOD

You are not who you used to be. In Christ, you have been made new. Your past does not define you, God does. Walk in the identity He has given you. *How can you live as the new creation God has made you?*

SHIELD OF FAITH

Lord, thank You for making me new. I leave behind my past and embrace the future You have for me. Help me to walk in the fullness of my new identity in Christ.

In Jesus name I pray, Amen.

1. How has your life changed since becoming a new creation in Christ?

_____

_____

_____

_____

_____

_____

_____

_____

_____

_____

2. What old habits or mindsets do you need to leave behind today?

_____

_____

_____

_____

_____

_____

_____

_____

_____

_____

3. Write a declaration embracing your identity as a new creation.

_____

_____

_____

_____

_____

_____

_____

_____

_____

Whispers from the Heart

This space is for your heart's dialogue with God. Whether it's a prayer, a reflection, a question, or a moment of gratitude—allow this area to capture what God is revealing to you in your journey. There are no rules here, just an open invitation to pour out your thoughts and listen for His whisper— from the One who knows you best.

Day 30

Freedom Through Christ

Sword of the Spirit

"Therefore if the Son makes you free, you shall be free indeed." – John 8:36 (NKJV)

Full Armor of God

Deliverance is your portion in Christ. He came to set you free from sin, bondage, and oppression. The chains that once held you have no power over you anymore. Walk in the freedom that Jesus paid for with His Blood. *How do you begin to live in the freedom Christ has given you?*

Shield of Faith

Jesus, I thank You for the freedom You purchased for me. I reject every lie of the enemy that tries to keep me bound. I declare that I am free indeed— free from sin, fear, and oppression. Help me to walk boldly in my deliverance.

In Jesus name I pray, Amen.

1. What does living in freedom through Christ look like for you?

_____

_____

_____

_____

_____

_____

_____

_____

_____

2. Reflect on a time when God delivered you from something that once held you captive.

_____

_____

_____

_____

_____

_____

_____

_____

_____

_____

3. Write a prayer thanking Jesus for the freedom He has given you.

_____

_____

_____

_____

_____

_____

_____

_____

_____

Whispers from the Heart

This space is for your heart's dialogue with God. Whether it's a prayer, a reflection, a question, or a moment of gratitude—allow this area to capture what God is revealing to you in your journey. There are no rules here, just an open invitation to pour out your thoughts and listen for His whisper— from the One who knows you best.

_____
_____
_____
_____
_____
_____
_____
_____
_____
_____
_____
_____
_____
_____
_____
_____
_____
_____
_____
_____
_____
_____
_____
_____

Words of Encouragement

Know that God is refining you, speaking to you, and preparing you for the amazing journey ahead. Keep pressing in, keep listening, and keep praying.

God is with you every step of the way.

The righteous cry out, and the Lord hears, and delivers them out of all their troubles.
– Psalm 34:17 (NKJV)

* * *

ABOUT THE AUTHOR

Jaun Malcolm– a licensed minister, intercessor, mentor, educator, author, and photographer– was born in Jamaica, W.I., and immigrated to the United States during her early years. From a young age, Jaun found solace in the arts, garnering accolades for her talents in drawing and writing. Her life has been marked by significant challenges, including a life-altering near-death experience in 2008, which deepened her faith and defined her life's purpose.

Inspired by Isaiah 61:1, Jaun is passionate about her calling to bring good tidings to the meek, heal the brokenhearted, and proclaim liberty to captives. She shares a powerful message of hope, redemption, and salvation, touching the lives of those ready to listen. With her profound grasp of the Scriptures, Jaun acts as a dedicated conduit for God, guiding others toward spiritual growth, transformation, and the fulfillment of God's promises for all Believers.